CW00419016

ETTON

A Village of the East Riding

by

Gail M. White

HUTTON PRESS

1992

Published by

The Hutton Press Ltd.,
130 Canada Drive, Cherry Burton, Beverley,
East Yorkshire HU17 7SB

Copyright © 1992

The first impression is a limited edition of 1250
copies of which the first 500 are numbered and
signed by the author.

No part of this book may be reproduced, stored in
a retrieval system or transmitted in any form,
photocopying, recording or otherwise without the
prior permission of the Publisher and the Copyright
holders.

Printed by

Clifford ward & Co. (Bridlington) Ltd.,
55 West Street, Bridlington, East Yorkshire
YO15 3DZ

ISBN 1 872167 42 X

CONTENTS

ACKNOWLEDGEMENTS

I am indebted to the many people who have helped me to produce this book, whether helping with research, giving permission to use extracts from both archive and published material or with the loan of photographs.

I would particularly like to thank the following people for their kindness, patience and valuable assistance: Adrian Havercroft, archaeological executor for the late Prof. W. J. Varley; Mary Varley, who, in talking about her late husband's work in Etton, inspired me to write this book; Brian Dyson, Hull University Archivist; J. G. W. Roberts, County Librarian; Miss Pamela Martin and staff at Beverley Local Studies Library; Staff at Hull Local Studies Library; Christopher Elrington, General Editor of the Victoria History of the Counties of England, for allowing me to use material from the series; Mrs. S. Thomas, West Yorkshire Archive Service; Edward Higgs, Search Department, Public Record Office, London; Mr. and Mrs. B. S. R. Rambaut; Revd. H. E. Hutchinson; Mr. K. D. Holt, County Archivist, and staff at the Humberside County Archive Office; staff at the Borthwick Institute of Historical Research; The East Yorkshire Federation of Women's Institutes; Revd. D. Austerberry; Mr. A. Lathrop; Misses M. and E. Sever; Misses M. and A. Welbourn; Mr. J. Duggleby; Mr. and Mrs. R. Moverley.

Gail M. White,
Etton
September 1992

PREFACE

As St. Mary's Church, Etton, is in great need of funds to preserve it for future generations, any royalties from the sale of this book will be donated to the Restoration Fund.

'Churches are the essential buildings of England. They are the visible sign of the continuity of our history. Almost everything else we have built is transient, liable to be replaced when it has ceased to be of use.
    A church is different. It is both ancient and modern. It is a monument to what went before and a promise of what is to come.'

Brian Redhead

Reproduced by kind permission of Brian Redhead (writer and broadcaster) and *Country Living* (Dec. 1991).

INTRODUCTION

Since moving to Etton 9 years ago, I gradually became aware that the village must have a fascinating history. Little did I realise just how interesting and how well documented the history is. Research opened the door to more and more information and so I decided that it would be worthwhile to bring together selected material in a simplified, and hopefully interesting form, together with photographs, maps and ephemera to help record the details.

It is not intended to be a definitive history of Etton — I will leave that to others more qualified than myself — but if it can awaken an awareness of the heritage which surrounds us, it will have served its purpose.

The village of Etton lies at the foot of the southern border of the Yorkshire Wolds, about five miles north-west of the town of Beverley. The houses are arranged on either side of the main street in a typical medieval 'street' layout, the village having changed remarkably little over the last few hundred years.

Etton has been fortunate in that there have been a number of interesting discoveries relating to its past. Some of these have been of major importance, such as the finding and subsequent translation of the seventy-four Etton land-charters, dating from 1170 — 1482, and the location of the site occupied bv the Knights Templar during the 13th to early 14th centuries.

In 1932 a *Yorkshire Post* journalist wrote that, 'It is always a boast of English historians that our records, both local and national, are the most complete in Europe.... It would be interesting to know, however, which village or town could boast the most complete historical records. It seems likely that this is a distinction which belongs to the East Yorkshire village of Etton.'

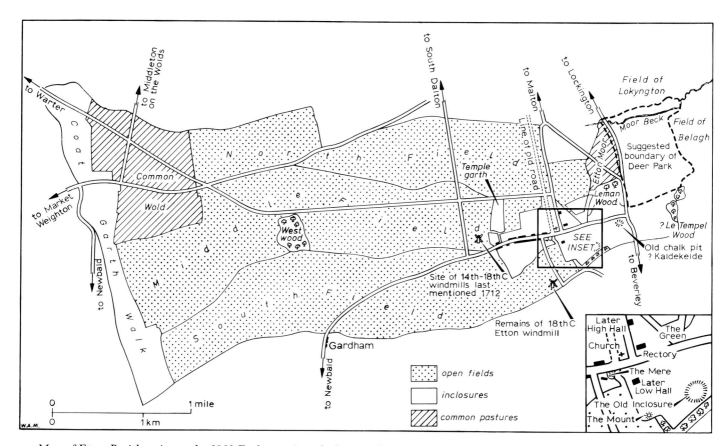

Map of Etton Parish, prior to the 1819 Enclosure Award, showing the sheep walk, common wold and open fields in the west of the parish and the suggested boundary of Etton deer Park* in the east. Some of the roads shown are post-enclosure.
* See: 'Medieval Parks of East Yorkshire' by Susan Neave (Hutton Press).
Map courtesy of Wendy Munday, Cartographer, Humberside University.

ETTON: A VILLAGE OF THE EAST RIDING

It is difficult to know exactly when the dry valley which became the site of the village of Etton was first settled. A small number of prehistoric features have been noted in the parish, on its western borders with the Wolds. These were 'tumuli' or burial mounds, containing skeletons, which were investigated by William Greenwell around 1860 and can be dated to the early Bronze Age, about 2,000-1,500 B.C.[1]

Two miles north of Gardham, several interesting finds were made, including a fine pottery burial urn, (now in the British Museum), pig bones and a bronze awl. One barrow contained the bodies of an adult woman, a child of about seven years of age, and with them, a superb flint knife.[2]

We then leap forward one and a half thousand years to Roman-occupied Britain, when life was far more sophisticated than anything known before. In 1874, on one of Lord Hotham's farms, then in the occupation of a Mr. Whipp, a large structure probably used for drying cereals was discovered, with two parallel walls of chalk and sandstone and a roof of sandstone slabs. Mixed in the soil, over and around it, were a large millstone, animal bones and pottery fragments, all apparently of Roman date.[3] The only other find of this date was a single piece of pot found in disturbed levels during the re-excavation of the burial mounds on Etton Wold in 1969-70.

Perhaps the most interesting archaeological discovery was that made by Professor Varley, distinguished archaeologist and resident of Etton, in 1965-66, when he located the site occupied by the Knights Templar in Etton during the 13th to early 14th centuries.[4] The Templars, who were a military religious order founded in 1118 between the first and second Crusades, undertook the task of protecting pilgrims during their travels to and from the Holy Land. They acquired their estates by grants from the Crown and other rich landowners, much of their property being located in the Midlands and North of the country, particularly in Yorkshire. Revenue from their estates, such as Temple Garth in Etton, which was partly acquired through the benevolence of the de Etton family[5], was used to further the Order throughout Christendom.

Temple Garth covers an area of some ten acres, just north of the main street and connected to it by a short grassy way known as Ellerington Lane. Excavations revealed a large 'furnagio' or great oven for malting barley, and it is known from inventories[6] which have survived that there was also a granary, kitchen, brew house or cellar, and chapel. We also know from these inventories, drawn up in 1307-8 and 1310, that the Templars kept numerous livestock, including a large flock of sheep and even a couple of peacocks. They also had an extensive acreage of crops such as wheat, barley, oats and peas.

During the 'dig', traces of the granary and the cobbled roadway were found, but one of the most interesting finds was a pitcher, now known as the Etton Vase, pieces of which were recovered from an ash pit near the oven. This has been described as 'a vessel of exceptionally good quality, covered with an ample green glaze, having thumb-pressed decoration on the handle, spout and base' with the *croix pommée* or equal-armed cross of the Templars impressed on to it, and dating from the late 13th century. Fixed into the cobbled roadway was a coin of Henry III, a half penny dated 1248-50 A.D. Both of these finds are now in the Hull Museum. The chapel was never found, but among the spoil after the site had been bulldozed level, schoolboy Stuart Rennie found a broken holy water stoup, now placed in a wall in the garden of 68 Main Street. The only surviving evidence of a mill was half a millstone ploughed up by Jim Kitchen during the Second World War, now forming a doorstep at the same house[7], once the home of Professor and Mrs. Varley.

The Templars obviously thrived in Etton and elsewhere during the 13th century, but they eventually came to be despised and mistrusted, resulting in the King (Edward II) reluctantly issuing a writ on 15 December 1307 for their

A panoramic view of the Templar site looking from the north west and taken in c.1966. The 'dig' was then quite advanced and the 'furnagio' or great oven can be seen in the foreground.
Photograph by Mary Varley.

The 'furnagio' or great oven, from the north, taken when excavation had been nearly completed.
Photograph by Mary Varley.

seizure throughout Yorkshire. The Templars in Etton were arrested on January 8 1308 by the Sheriff of York, accompanied by about twenty men, and taken to York Castle for trial[8]. They were accused of holding midnight ceremonies, practising black magic, heresy and blasphemy. One witness reportedly said that the boys of Etton were told 'beware the kiss of the Templar' and that one of the women who did their washing said that they had the sign of the cross embroidered on their underwear! The Templars repudiated any form of heresy of which they had been accused and following several trials they were then distributed among the monasteries in the custody of the Church. Pensions of four pence a day were granted to them from their sequestrated estates, and from those which were eventually transferred to the Knights of St. John Hospitaller[9].

On May 5 1312 the Order of the Knights Templar officially ceased to exist. Pope Clement V issued a document for the confiscation of their entire property and ordered its transference to the Hospitallers, an order originally founded for the care of sick and wounded crusaders. The Hospitallers did not gain the estate in Etton, however, until around 1324, Temple Garth having first been granted to David, Earl of Athol, by King Edward II on February 8 1312:

> 'To Alexander de Cave and Robert de Amecotes, Keepers of the Templars' Lands in County York, Order to deliver to David, Earl of Athole, to whom the King has granted the Custody of the Templars' Manors of Etton and Cave in that County during Pleasure, the Corn in the same Manors and the Custody of the Ornaments of the Chapel, and the Implements and other Goods in the said Manors, together with the Stock there.[10]'

Original Settlement

It has been suggested that the original Domesday village of Etton was located to the east of Low Hall, an area now covered with earthworks which stand out clearly under the grass. This site, known as the 'Old Enclosure', was partially excavated by W. J. Varley in 1967, and consists of an earthwork of probably late 13th to early 14th century date, which overlays occupation material of the earlier village of Etton.[11] Several iron arrowheads and horseshoes were discovered at the site, probably indicating an involvement with hunting. Just to the north of Low Hall is a mound, the use of which is uncertain, possibly a vantage point, or perhaps the base of an old windmill.

Domesday Survey

Apart from the archaeological evidence of Etton's past, there is also written evidence, the earliest of this being the Domesday Survey ordered by William the Conqueror, and compiled between 1085 and 1087. The main entries for Etton are as follows:

Land of Archbishop of York:

> In Ettone eight carucates to be taxed, and there may be four ploughs. This manor was, and is, St. John's (Beverley). Eight villeins have there five ploughs. Value in King Edward's time ten shillings, at present eight shillings.

Land of the Count de Mortain:

> In Steitorp (the location of this is unknown) and Etton, Turchil had two manors, of seven carucates and six oxgangs to be taxed, and there may be five ploughs, Nigel has in his demesne one plough: and seven villeins and one bordar and one plough and a half. Wood pasture half a league long and the same broad. Value in King Edward's time fifty shillings, at present twenty shillings.

Land of Hugh, son of Baldric:

> Two manors, in Ettone Gamel had nine carucates of land and two oxgangs to be taxed. There is land for five ploughs. Hugh, a vassal of Hugh's hath now there two ploughs, and ten villeins and two bordars with one plough. Value in King Edward's time forty shillings, now the same.

Carucate — The amount of land which could be tilled in a year by one plough and 8 oxen.

Oxgang — An eighth of a carucate.

Demesne — Land farmed by the Lord of the Manor.

Villein — Peasant with land in the common fields.

Bordar — Peasant without land in the common fields: a smallholder.

The cntry for Etton makes no mention of a church or mill, so it is probable that these were both built immediately after the great survey.

The Downe Papers

A major source of written evidence for the history of Etton from 1170 to 1482 is a collection of manuscripts known as the Downe Papers. This consists of land-charters, quitclaims and leases discovered 'in the dark recesses of a strong-room, in the ancient city of York'. Written in Latin and Norman French, these papers belonging to the family of Viscount Downe, of Wykeham Abbey, Yorkshire, were painstakingly translated by the eminent historian, T. Walter Hall and were published by him in 1932.[12] They give a unique glimpse of Etton's medieval history and particularly of the family de Etton and their successors the Langdales.

Geoffrey de Etton, father of Thomas de Etton, the elder, was the son of Edward de Mawnsell, a French knight, who must have reached Yorkshire soon after the Norman conquest of 1066. This Geoffrey, and many of his descendants, are referred to in the Etton charters.

What appears to be the earliest of these is a grant, dated c.1170, from William Fossard to Thomas, son of Geoffrey de Etton, of a spring of water, which was called Kaldekelde, meaning cool spring or cold well, to supply the mill-pond of Etton. (This is the first mention of a mill). For this grant, which included land, Thomas had to pay to William one clove gillyflower yearly.

Deer parks were quite common in East Yorkshire in medieval times and the situation of a park at Etton is referred to in several charters. At some time during the reign of Henry II (1154-89), Thomas de Etton, the elder, obtained a royal licence 'to have and hold his park, which he had made in his lands at Etton, just as he had enclosed it, well wholly and in peace; and he forbade anyone, without the licence of the said Thomas, to enter and chase deer there or take away any deer.'

This licence gave Thomas security of title to his land and it passed down through the family for a period of about 140 years to Laurence de Etton, who named the park 'Laurence Park'.

The park is described in a later charter of 1309 as 'lying in length between the field of Lokyngton on the north and the park which was called le Tempel Wod on the south; and in breadth between the common moor of Etton west and the meadow of John Danyel and the field of Belagh on the east'. The park must therefore have been sited in the north-east corner of the parish.

Laurence de Etton finally handed the estate to his second daughter, Amanda, this leading to many family quarrels and misunderstandings, some of which were taken to the King's court. A number of charters granting land between Laurence de Etton and his children reveal that payments were made, not in money, but by the rather delightful token gesture of 'a pair of gloves at the feast of Pentecost' or 'a rose in the time of roses'.

In the early 14th century Amanda married Patrick de Langdale and from this time onwards he took control of his wife's lands, including Laurence Park, and became the chief man of Etton.

The estate descended in the Langdale family until the 18th century, when under the terms of the Langdale Estate Act it was sold to Frances, the widow of Sir Thomas Legard, Bt, the lands then passing to the Hotham family in 1862.[13]

An indenture of lease dated January 20 1412 (13) made between Thomas Langedayle of Etton and John Richardson and Richard his son of Wetwang, testified that Thomas granted his manor of Etton and several acres of land to the Richardsons for a term of nine years. They were to 'well and properly maintain amend and repair the roof,

An undated Charter, probably c.1170, in Latin. Confirms a grant from William Fossard to Thomas son of Geoffrey de Etton of a spring of water which was called 'Kaldekelde'.
Reproduced from *Etton an East Yorkshire Village - Time 1170 to 1482* by T. Walter Hall by kind permission of the Rt. Hon. the Viscount Downe. Original document held at North Yorkshire County Record Office, Northallerton, as part of the *Dawnay Archive*.

thatch and walls in the aforesaid manor, at their own cost; the hall and chamber with the tiled roof only excepted ... and the aforesaid Thomas and his heirs were to provide timbers for the maintenance of the manor ... further it should be lawful for the aforesaid John and Richard ... to fell and cut yearly a hundred faggots of thorn, there growing for his fuel.'

In St. Mary's Church, Etton, there lies what remains of a broken stone effigy of a woman, said to be Leonora Langdale, which formerly showed three small shields, 'one of which bears the arms of Frevile, a name often occurring as a witness in the Etton charters'.[14] Patrick Langdale, husband of Amanda (formerly de Etton), was buried in the Chapel Chancel of the parish of Etton in 1357.

Medieval Etton

The village of Etton has a typical medieval layout; the houses and farmsteads extending along the main street with gardens running back from them — the old tofts and crofts. At one time all the houses would have been thatched, but gradually these were replaced with the brick and tiled buildings which can be seen today.

Early medieval farming methods meant that a village had a small number of very large fields, one or two being kept fallow, while the others were cultivated, all in rotation. Each villager had several strips of land allocated to him, these being scattered between the fields so that everyone had a share of both good and poor land. Grazing land was held in common and subject to strict rules and regulations.

In the mid-12th century there were 195 acres of arable land in open fields to the west of the village, and by the end of the 14th century this became known as West Field. East Field was mentioned some 50 years earlier with rough grazing being found on the moor north-east of the village and on the higher wolds to the west. In the 16th century the Knights Hospitaller owned the Eastwood and the adjoining Westwood, comprising about 60 acres. Large numbers of sheep were kept on the estates of both the Hospitallers and Watton Priory, and the latter had a

sheep-walk in Etton (Cotegarth Walk) by 1275. By the 17th century there were three open fields, North, South and Middle Fields, and these remained until the time of enclosure in 1820.[15]

Medieval Etton had a rather different road pattern from that which we see today. Main Street, formerly called Town Street, which extends from east to west through the village, had long been in existence, but other roads are comparatively new and yet others long abandoned.

The former course of a road running north from the main street can be found behind Church Farm, to the west of the church. The track can be seen clearly as a depression in the field and excavations have shown that the ancient cobbles still lie not far below the surface.[16] There are earthworks on both sides of the road which may mark the sites of former houses. A cul-de-sac beside the pond is all that remains of the old course of the Cherry Burton Road, then known as Marr or Mere Lane. It was moved westwards at the time of enclosure in 1820 and later renamed New Road. The eastern end of Etton formerly lay round a wedge-shaped green which probably extended as far as the moor in the east of the parish. The Etton manuscripts refer to the de la Grene family in the 13th and 14th centuries — they presumably lived near the green.[17]

Justice

Medieval justice could be both harsh and cruel; no evidence of this survives in Etton, but undoubtedly justice would have been meted out in the same way as anywhere else. The earliest surviving jury verdicts for the manor court of Etton date from 1694[18]. The court obviously regulated the life of the parish quite effectively, as the following verdicts show:

1694 — *14 people fined for staking their horses on the common balks.*

Dux gooing in the marr (Pond) – William Lyon –4d.

Several people fined 8d. for allowing their swine on the green.

An Indenture of Lease (Latin) dated at Beverley on January 20th, 1412-13, testifying that Thomas Langedayle
of Etton granted his manor of Etton to John Richardson and Richard his son of Wetwang, for nine years.
*Prior to September 1752, the civil or legal year in England commenced on the 25th March, whilst the historical year
began as at present, on the 1st January. Confusion was therefore created in describing the year between
the 1st January and the 25th March, as civilians called each day within that period of time one year earlier than historians;
e.g. the former wrote January 20th, 1412, and the latter wrote January 20th, 1413, though both described the
25th of the following March, and all the following months as being in the year 1413.
Reproduced from Etton an East Yorkshire Village - Time 1170 to 1482 by
T. Walter Hall by kind permission of the Rt. Hon. the Viscount Downe. Original document held at
North Yorkshire County Record Office, Northallerton, as part of the Dawnay Archive.*

1714 — *William Elliot of South Dalton for baiting and tethering in ye field of Etton – 1s 6d.*

1727 — *Sir Thomas Legard bart. for his ducks anoying ye Marre – 3d.*

Philip Langdale Esq. for not doing suite and service at this court – £1 19s 0d.

1730 — *Mathew Husley for having a scabbed horse in the field – 1s.*

John Hodgson for not cutting his wood next the Marr Lane – 4d.

1731 — *3 servants for riding over the corn with their horses – 1 fined 1s, 2 fined 4d.*

1733 — *Wallis Johnson for not reading the Pains (the list of rules and regulations) – 1d.*

1743 — *J. Woodcroft for thrashing corn by candlelight contrary to Pains – 2d.*

1746 — *Thomas Butler for his pigs unsty'd in the night – 1d.*

In 1836 an interesting case was recorded in the register of burials[19] by Revd. Robert Machell, the coroner's certificate being pasted over the entry:

William Drewery of Etton, aged 62 years — poisoned.

Revd. Machell writes at the foot of the page, with obvious satisfaction, that his son William 'was tried at York but was acquitted. He afterwards emigrated to America with his father's property — £500 — and returned a pauper after a very short time'.

Enclosure

The medieval system of strip farming disappeared during the 18th and 19th centuries as fields were enclosed to improve the efficiency and productivity of the countryside. An ever-growing urban population needed more and more food to sustain it.

An Act was drawn up to enclose land in Etton in 1818[20] and the execution of the Enclosure Award was proclaimed in the village on 13 August 1820. The enclosure plan[21] shows the new road which was made to Cherry Burton, and how the land was allotted to the various owners. The land concerned amounted to 2,812 acres, and this was mainly divided between Robert Belt, Lord Hotham, Sir Thomas Legard, Bt. and the Revd. John Gilby.

The Hotham estate in Etton originated in 1783 when William Hotham, later Baron Hotham, bought 236 acres from the Revd. Abraham Rudd. This was added to in 1820, at the time of enclosure, by purchases totalling 638 acres and in 1831 increased substantially by a purchase of 1,335 acres from Robert Belt.[22] Lord Hotham had been anxious to enlarge his estate in the area and to this end his agent, John Hall of Scorborough, was urged to buy land. The opportunity to purchase Robert Belt's estate presented itself when the property was put up for auction on 30 July 1830.[23] It included the farm known as Wallis Grange, then occupied by a Mr. John Richardson; the Blacksmith's house and workshop; a Public House, presumably the Light Dragoon Inn; and several other properties. The sale price for the estate was £35,000, with an agreement that the purchase would be completed on 1 January 1831.

By 1872, Charles, Lord Hotham, had 2,967 acres in Etton, and in December, 1991 the Hotham estate owned 2,424 acres in the parish.[24]

St. Mary's Church, Etton

The church at Etton dates from about 1150, with a rector, 'Ivo', being mentioned in the year 1200. The Revd. Robert Machell, Curate in charge of Etton from 1834-54, wrote[25] that 'the church which is dedicted to St. Mary, is built upon an eminence at the eastern extremity of the village, and approached from the south it is a striking object. Its general appearance is picturesque, for the massive Norman tower, seen amongst the trees, shews like the keep of an old castle of ye anglo saxon period...' This western tower contains three bells, the tenor bell dating back to c.1400. It was an ancient custom for the clerk to receive 'a sheaf of wheat and a sheaf of barley for each oxgang in the fields for ringing the bell each day at Harvest at 5 o'clock in the morning and 7 o'clock in the evening.'[26]

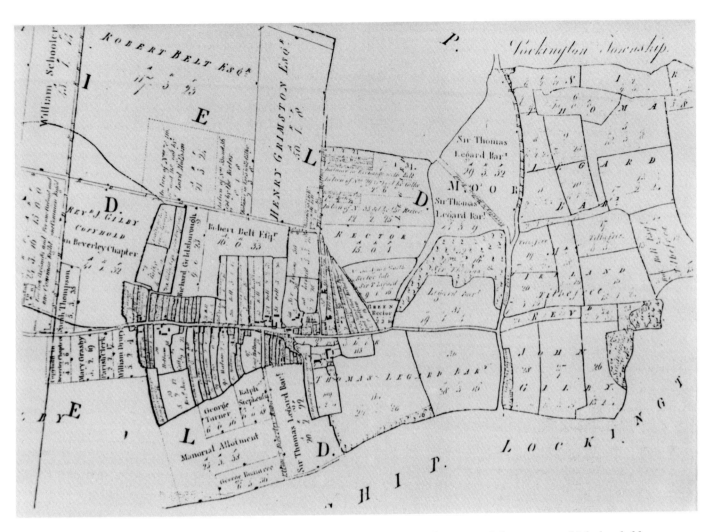

Part of the Etton Enclosure Award Map (1819) showing names of landowners and the acreages which they held.
Reproduced by kind permission of Humberside Record Office and Etton Parish Council.

A notice announcing the sale, by auction, of Robert Belt's estate in Etton in 1830, giving a vivid description of the parish at this time. The 'excellent roads' to which it refers were probably far from the standard to which we are accustomed today! The entire estate was later sold to Lord Hotham for £35,000.
Reproduced by kind permission of Lord Hotham and Hull University Library. Ref. H.U.L. DDHO 30/93.

YORKSHIRE.

PARTICULARS OF A MOST VALUABLE
FREEHOLD ESTATE,

Situate in the Township and Parish of **ETTON**, within Four Miles of
BEVERLEY,

In a good Neighbourhood, with excellent Roads, and in a fine Sporting Part of the East Riding of the County of York;

CONSISTING OF

THREE VALUABLE FARMS,

With superior Farm Houses and Agricultural Out Buildings,

ALSO,

A Public House and several Cottages with Garths and Orchards in the Village of Etton;

COMPRISING IN THE WHOLE UPWARDS OF

1335 Acres

OF

EXCELLENT LAND,

And Occupied by most respectable Yearly Tenants at reduced Rents to meet the exigencies of the Times.

The Estate is situate within Four Miles of the Market Town of *Beverley*, within Thirteen of *Hull*, and Six of *Market Weighton*. It adjoins upon the well-preserved Estates of LORD HOTHAM and SIR THOMAS LEGARD, Bart., is well stocked with Game, and Two Packs of Hounds are kept in the Neighbourhood.

The Estate is subject to a Corn Rent in lieu of Tithes, which was fixed by the Etton Inclosure Act, and will be variable in the Year 1834, when a Reduction in the Amount of such Corn Rent may fairly be expected. The Parochial Rates are very Moderate.

THIS ELIGIBLE PROPERTY
Will be Sold by Auction

AT THE

GEORGE INN, CONEY STREET, YORK,

On FRIDAY, the 30th Day of JULY, 1830, at Twelve o'Clock at Noon,

IN ONE LOT,

Or in the following, or such other Lots as may be agreed upon at the Time of Sale.

For further Particulars application must be made to MR. ROBINSON, *Essex Street, Strand, London;* MESSRS. BROOK and BULMER, *Solicitors, York;* MESSRS. SHEPHERD and MYERS, *Solicitors, Beverley; or* MR. WARE, *Skirpenbeck, York.*

Eminent ecclesiastics have frequently held the position of Rector at St. Mary's, but many of these were not resident in the parish. At least two royal clerks were rectors in the 14th century,[27] one of these being John of Etton (?John Hotham)[28], who later became Chancellor of the Exchequer in 1331.

The richly carved tower arch is one of the finest examples of 12th-century stonework in the whole of Yorkshire, and the semi-circular-headed west doorway has an interesting series of recessed mouldings depicting birds' heads. The tower arch was formerly hidden by a west gallery and Revd. Machell remarks in his notes (c.1843) that 'this beautiful Norman Arch, which divides the tower from the Nave is at present nearly concealed by an immence (*sic*) wooden gallery, erected in Mr. Fox's time, about 80 years ago, nothing but actual want of room suffers it to remain as it holds between 60 and 70 persons ... Altogether this is one of the most admirable Norman arches and I hope the time will soon come, when its beauties will be brought to light, and the falling building be restored (if not to its original grandeur) to its former security — it is now insecure, and when the bells are ringing, dangerous.'

Revd. Machell did eventually get his wish, for in 1867-8 work was carried out which included removing the west gallery, rebuilding the tower, re-roofing the nave and adding the north vestry.

During an earlier restoration in 1844, an old stone was discovered[29] when workmen demolished the entire north wall. Now placed in the centre of the new wall, the stone depicts what is thought to be the arms of the de Mauley family, who were associated with the Knights Templar in Etton during the 13th century.

Another interesting feature is the 'Wake Knot' below the piscina, situated in the south wall to the right of the altar and also discovered in 1844 when the chancel wall was pulled down. In the time of King John (1199-1216), William de Stuteville (or Estouteville) held the Manor of Cottingham with its Knight's fee in Etton, having inherited the estate from his ancestor, Robert de Stuteville,

Sheriff of York. His great granddaughter, Joan, married into the family de Wake, and the Manor passed to her son and heir Baldwin de Wake. The name Estouteville, originating from the Norman knights, can be found on a window on the north side of the chancel, commemorating Henry Estouteville Grimston of Etton. The Grimston family were resident at High Hall, Etton, during the 19th and early 20th centuries.

A recent addition is the memorial stone placed on the north wall commemorating the baptism of John Lowthrop at Etton, during the reign of Queen Elizabeth I, on December 20 1584. Revd. Lowthrop is revered by many Americans as one of their first spiritual leaders.

After graduating from Cambridge University, John Lowthrop was ordained into the Church of England, his first appointment being at Bennington, Hertfordshire, followed by the post of Perpetual Curate at Egerton in Kent.[30]

He later resigned his curacy to become minister of the Independent Church in Southwark, London. This brought him into conflict with Charles I's High Church Archbishop of Canterbury, the unpopular William Laud.

John Lowthrop was arrested and tried before Archbishop Laud, but was eventually released on condition that he did not preach or hold meetings. In 1634 he courageously gathered together some of his congregation and set sail for the New World on board the *Griffin*.

That journey into the unknown, even with the horrors of the Atlantic sea voyage, was simply the lesser of two evils. This little band of faithful Christians was one of the earliest to settle in the New World. The Pilgrim Fathers had sailed from Plymouth in the *Mayflower* to found the first colony in New England in 1620, but William Penn, the famous Quaker and founder of Pennsylvania, was not to be born until 1644, ten years after the Revd. Lowthrop had landed at Boston.

John Lowthrop's daughter, Jane, accompanied her father on the voyage and was subsequently married to Samuel Fuller who had come on the *Mayflower* as a boy. Their marriage was performed by another famous pilgrim, Miles Standish.[31]

These two photographs show the interior of St. Mary's Church, Etton: before the restoration of 1867 (left) and after (right). The west gallery was removed, revealing the splendour of the Norman archway and a royal coat of arms appears on the wall above it. New roof beams were installed along with a new pulpit; the old box pews were replaced; the flooring improved and lighting installed in the form of candelabra – no electricity in those days! Electricity did not come to Etton until about 1936.

Boston was a puritan place, not sharing the separatist ideas of the Lowthrop group, so shortly after landing they proceeded down the coast to Scituate, Plymouth Colony. In 1639, however, because of dissension relating to baptismal matters and lack of sufficient grazing land, Revd. Lowthrop and his followers moved to the base of Cape Cod, to what is now Barnstable, Massachusetts. Upon their arrival the flock celebrated communion at what is now preserved as Sacrament Rock.

John Lowthrop died in 1652, leaving 12 children and many grandchildren, so it is understandable that the extended family of Lowthrops is numerous and encompasses many famous names. They include Henry Longfellow, Franklin D. Roosevelt, Adlai Stevenson, Ulysses Grant, Joseph Smith, the founder of the Mormon Church, and last but not least, George Bush, 41st President of the United States of America.[32]

Non-Conformity

In 1597 William Anlaby of Etton was executed for the crime of being a Roman Catholic missionary priest. The Protestant Queen, Elizabeth I, was then on the throne, and although reasonably tolerant of people with opposing religious views, she expected them to maintain outward signs of conformity. During the reign of her successor, James I, in 1605-6, Thomas Babthorpe and three others, of Etton, were fined for refusing to attend Anglican services.[33]

In 1845 the Primitive Methodists built a chapel in Etton and this boasted a strong following among the villagers in the late 19th and early 20th centuries. The chapel, situated in the centre of the village on the south side of Main Street, was closed in 1968 and later converted into a private garage attached to the house now known as Chapel House.

Parish Registers

The longest continuous records of family histories in Etton are the parish registers, and these survive from 1557. In 1598, Elizabeth I instructed that old parish registers should be copied onto parchment and it is this first parchment register which is the earliest surviving record of baptisms, marriages and burials in Etton.[34]

In this first register can be found the names of two families whose subsequent generations have survived to this day. One of these is the Lowthrop family which is now distributed over the entire United States of America and whose history has been mentioned earlier. There appear to be sixteen entries in this register for christenings of members of the Lowthrop family when they lived in Etton. One of these is John Lowthrop, on December 20 1584, son of Thomas Lowthrop. This is the John Lowthrop who later became so renowned as a spiritual leader in the New World.

The other family, who can list over one hundred entries in this register, is that of Owstaby, later to become known as Austerberry and widely scattered throughout America, Australia and here in England. Indeed, many pages of the Etton Register were witnessed by William Owstaby as Guardian (presumably similar to a churchwarden). An early reference to the Owstaby name occurs in the Etton manuscripts, which mention Robert Ousteby as being a tenant of land in Etton in 1482. An even earlier reference, but not fully substantiated as being in Etton, is from the Yorkshire Pipe Rolls for 1230 which records a Hugo Oustiby of Aton (possibly Etton) who paid 12 pence tax!

The most notable member of the Owstaby family was John Ostaby, fellow of Pembroke College, Cambridge from 1498 and Chaplain-Librarian of Cambridge University from 1510-22.[35] He was succeeded in this important position by two famous figures in history, Latimer and Ridley, both burnt to death as Protestant heretics in 1555.

The Owstaby name is Old Norse in origin and it must be assumed that they came during the Viking invasions in the 9th century. The name Østerby is still found in Denmark, Norway and Sweden today.

Charities

Bequests benefiting the parishioners of Etton date back to the early 18th century. It was at this time that Mr. Towers

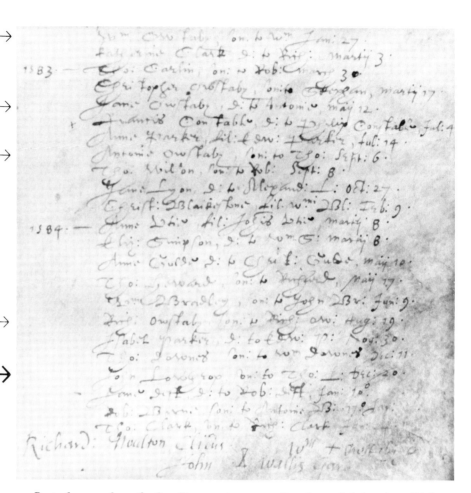

Etton's first Parish Register recorded on parchment. It records: Marriages from 1560-1664; Christenings from 1557-1664; Burials from 1557-1663 Now kept at Humberside Record Office, Beverley. Photo by kind permission of Humberside Record Office.

Part of a page from the first Etton register recording dates of christenings. Light arrows – Owstaby family; Dark arrow x John Lowthrop. Signed by Richard Houlton, Clerk, and marked with a cross by William Owstaby and John Wallis, Guardians. Obviously, the latter were unable to write their names, as was common amongst the majority of the population at the time. Photo by kind permission of Humberside Record Office.

Wallis, late Alderman of Hull (d.1719) and Mr. Benjamin Ealand of Etton left £60 between them, which was used to purchase a small estate, comprising a cottage, garth and four acres at Faxfleet (in South Cave). The income, of five guineas per annum, was used to buy bread, which was distributed amongst the poor of the parish every Sunday. The Common Right belonging to the estate was later sold off for £40, to which the Revd. John Fox, Rector 1780-1816, added £50 and Frances Legard £10, this sum being invested in stock, with the income of £4 per annum, in 1799, being distributed four times a year.[36]

A further benefactor to the village was Mr. William Wilson. Robert Machell (Curate 1834-54) left copious notes[37] on the village, its residents and the church, and among these he tells that William Wilson 'never indulged in any relaxation, and when compelled to ride to Beverley to market, he never used a saddle or put his horse up. He regularly purchased 16 loaves for which he paid a shilling a week, and gave to the poor what remained after his wants were satisfied.' He died on July 22 1816, aged 72 years, and was buried in Beverley where he had lived during the latter part of his life — he had previously farmed in Etton.

A memorial in Etton Church reveals the details of his will, in which he left £400 to the Parish of St. John in Beverley, £400 to the Parish of St. Mary, also in Beverley, and £200 to the Parish of Etton. These sums of money were to be used for the purchase of white bread to be given on Sundays to the poor of the respective parishes. He left a further £400 to Beverley Corporation for the benefit and promotion of the Boys' Charity School in Beverley.

Parishioners in Etton also benefited from the will of Mrs. Jane Legard[38] of Etton, dated 24 November 1835. An extract from this will reads:

'To the Resident Rector or Curate of Etton.
I leave in trust to be placed in the 'Savings Bank, Beverley, Forty Pounds', the money to be supplied as wanted to keep in good repair or when wanted to renew, in three sets of Child Bed Articles, now let to the poor married women, living in Etton during their confinement.

The 'Etton National Schoolmistress' for the Girls to have the care of the Child Bed Articles, and to let them out as wanted. The Girls of the School to assist in making and mending the Child Bed Articles.

The Schoolmistress to make some good gruel to send three times to each Woman while she has use of the Articles.

The Mistress to be allowed three Shillings a Quarter for her trouble.

The money for that, and the ingredients for the Gruel to be provided out of the Legacy left as above.

The 'Wife' of the 'resident Clergyman' is requested to see the Child Bed Articles properly attended to, and the money laid out to the best advantage.

N.B. The Child Bed Articles not to be lent until the Woman has been married nine months.

(Signed) Jane Legard

This Charity was known as the 'Etton Lying-in Charity'.

Obviously these bequests were of great benefit to those in need in the village, but they became rather antiquated as the years progressed. So, in 1973, these three charities were updated and brought together as 'Etton Relief in Need'[39], approved by the Charity Commissioners for England and Wales, and administered by a group of trustees drawn from the parish of Etton.

NOTABLE BUILDINGS

The Rectory

From the Etton Terriers, or inventories of church property, we know that rectors at Etton received all manner of tithes (traditionally one tenth of a person's income) and in 1685 these were paid in kind with hay, corn, fruit, geese, pigs, turkeys, chickens, ducks, bees, pigeons, wood etc.[40]

The Etton Terriers, of which 13 survive from 1685-1817, give excellent descriptions of the Rectory or 'Parsonage House' at Etton. The original house probably began in medieval times as a simple two-celled timber building, consisting of a main hall with open fire and adjoining

Copy of the Etton Terrier (inventory of church property) for 1685,
signed by Arthur Dalgarno, Rector from 1676-1731.
Reproduced by kind permission of
The Borthwick Institute of Historical Research.

service rooms, which form the basis of the present central range.[41]

In 1685 the Parsonage House consisted of 'a hall, a parlour, a fore kitchen, a back kitchen, and three little office rooms and pantries, one larder, a room commonly called the coal house. There are above stair four lodging chambers, one closett, a garret, with a room over the kitchen called a corn chamber.'[42] In 1764 the house is described as being built of brick and timber and being largely covered with tiles and partly with thatch.[43] The fabric of the Rectory was neglected for several years about this time, and in 1783, Revd. John Fox set about considerable extensions and improvements to the building. The Terrier of 1817[44] mentions 'one mefsuage or dwelling house built with brick and tile, the rooms within are two dining rooms with boarded floors, and hung with paper, two kitchens, one floored with flags, the other with bricks. One store room and wine cellar within, one dairy, one cellar, one butler's pantry, all floored with brick, one outhouse adjoining and also servants' hall with stove and fireplace, staircase and chamber over it, with boarded floor. Also a good brew house and place to clean knives and shoes in. Seven chambers, five of them hung with paper, one garret, one new barn built with brick and tile consisting of three small bays. One stable with two stands adjoining the same, with a pigeon chamber over it. One other stable with four stands, built with brick and tile, with a hay chamber over it, and all in good and sufficient repair and likewise rebuilt by the Revd. John Fox. And also a well, with two buckets, sunk near the house in 1809. One cottage (now taken down by permission of the late Archbishop in 1784 and an open stable with helm over it built there instead thereof) and Garth adjoining the church yard with Rights of Common as also the Parsonage House, according to the customs of the place. One garden and orchards, fenced on part by a brick wall, on the other part by a quickset hedge, one small close adjoining which with the garden, Orchard and Yard contains about 2 acres.'

On Saturday April 21 1888, the *Beverley Recorder and General Advertiser* recorded[45] an:

ALARMING ACCIDENT
AT ETTON
FALL OF A FLOOR AT THE RECTORY
SEVERAL PERSONS INJURED

On Tuesday afternoon the furniture etc., belonging to the late Rev. Canon Vernon was put up by auction at the Rectory, Etton, by Mr. Henry Sugdon, the sale being under the management of Messrs. Elwell and Son, of Beverley, and as several articles of value and a quantity of old wines, etc., were included a large number of people from Beverley and Hull, as well as from the adjacent villages, attended. All went well as the lots in the several bedrooms were knocked down, and about 370 had been disposed of, the next move – about half-past four o'clock – being to the schoolroom, in which had been arranged a pianoforte, cabinet, ottoman, various tables, and an assortment of nick-nacks such as ladies usually seek after. About fifty persons were already in the room, and as the auctioneer approached a rush was made by those who accompanied him, the bulk of the newcomers hurrying to the centre of the room. In a moment, and without warning, there was a loud crack, and the bulk of the people, together with the furniture, fell through the floor into the kitchen below. Very fortunately the floor did not give way at the sides, or the result must have been frightful. It seems as though the occupants of the room were all forced to a hole in the centre, as if passing through a hopper, and they piled one upon another until there was a nearly solid mass of six or seven deep.

As soon as the people outside and in the other portions of the house realised what had occurred the work of rescue commenced, but as all the kitchen doors but one opened inwardly they were blocked and the large window fronting the lawn was therefore broken away.

How heartily and systematically the rescuers worked may be judged from the fact that in about a quarter of an hour the whole of the occupants of the kitchen had been got out, and those who had been injured the most were tenderly placed upon the lawn.

There were some exceedingly narrow escapes. The kitchen was being used as a pay room, and here Mr. Wm. Elwell was receiving money, the only other occupants at the time of the accident being Mr. Gabbetis, butcher, of Beverley, and a youth, son of Mr. J. E. Elwell. They saw dust fall from the ceiling, and apprehending that something was wrong made a dash for the window, which gave way and they got out just before the floor fell in. How near they had been to injury, may be judged when we state that the chair on which Mr. Elwell sat and the table on which he had his accounts, were both reduced to fragments. It happened that these were immediately beneath the part of the floor which remained, but the people and the furniture as they descended filled up nearly every nook and corner of the kitchen.

The cause of the accident became apparent when the debris was examined. It seems that the floor of the room, which was not particularly large, was supported by two oaken beams. One of these, not strong enough to resist the pressure which followed the rush of people from the bedrooms and landing, broke in the centre, and the joists 'housed' into it also broke, the whole floor with the exception previously mentioned then giving way. The pianoforte and other heavy furniture gradually slid along and no doubt caught against the wall or other supports before falling on the people below. It was noticed that those most seriously injured were found near these articles.

The most serious case was that of Mrs. Gabbetis of Etton, who was seated on the pianoforte stool before the accident occurred. It was at once seen that this lady, who is in middle life, was severely hurt, and after resting for a time on the lawn she was removed home on a mattress.

The Rectory was taken over by the army during the Second World War and was later divided into two, the east wing (now demolished) housing retired clergy. The building was sold in 1965 and is now a private house — a new rectory was built just to the east of the former in 1964/65.[46]

Low Hall

Low Hall, now the home of the Holderness Hunt Kennels, was known as Etton Hall in 1771, Old Hall in 1832 and Low Hall since at least 1852. The surviving buildings, situated opposite Chantry Lane, include, to the west of the house site, a much-altered late-17th-century domestic range ending in a later three-storeyed tower, and to the north-east, a range of earlier 17th-century outbuildings. Old stone gateways of the late 17th to early 18th centuries can still be seen in sections of the brick enclosure walls to the side of the present house. Now part of the Hotham estate, Low Hall was formerly owned by the Legard family and before them the Estofts. In the hearth-tax returns of 1672, it is John Estoft's manor-house (Low Hall) which is recorded as having fifteen hearths.[47]

The Holderness Hunt at Etton

The kennels at Low Hall have been the headquarters of the Holderness Hunt since at least 1844.[48]

A pack of hounds was first formed in the Holderness area in 1726, but continuous hunting in the district did not begin until 1815, when Mr. Digby Legard of Etton kennelled 'a scratch pack' of hounds in the village. Mr. Legard improved the area considerably by planting numerous gorse coverts and his huntsman, Nailor, was said to have declared that 'you could hunt a fox with an old sow and a litter of pigs'! Owing to his state of health, Mr. Legard had to retire in 1821, the hounds being sold to a Mr. William Hay, who hunted them for just one season and then moved to Warwickshire.

In 1824, Mr. Tom Hodgson came to Beverley, living in modest quarters at the Rose and Crown, where he also kennelled his hounds for a while before moving them to what is now known as Dog Kennel Lane near Bishop Burton. He was said to have provided excellent sport in

Etton Rectory, from the south-west, in about 1930. In 1947 the house was divided, with the eastern wing being made into a separate house, called St. Mary's House. This eastern wing was later demolished in about 1965 when the Rectory was sold.
When the Rev. J. B. Cholmely was rector from 1914-37, his wife ran a small private boarding school at the Rectory. The children were often seen in the village with a teacher in charge of them and the village children were invited to see their plays, which were sometimes performed on the Rectory lawn.

The Etton Vase – this pitcher, 18½ inches (470 mm) in height, dating from the late 13th century, has been described as 'a vessel of exceptionally good quality, covered with an ample green glaze, having thumb-pressed decoration on the handle, spout and base' with the 'croix pommée' or equal-armed cross of the Templars impressed on to it. Broken pieces of the pitcher were discovered during archaeological excavations which were carried out at Temple Garth, Etton, in 1965/66. It is believed to be a copy, in pottery, of an earlier metal vessel.

Photograph by kind permission of Hull City Museums and Art Galleries.

A rare, medieval, hammered silver Short Cross penny of the time of King John (1199-1216), discovered, in mint condition, 2 years ago in Etton parish. (Magnification x 4).
The Short Cross penny takes its name from the reverse type, a cross with short arms, and remained the same in design until 1247. Even though it was issued by 4 different kings (Henry II, Richard I, John, Henry III) the king's name on the coin always read HENRICVS. Short cross coins can be attributed to chronological groups according to the details of the design and lettering. This coin was struck between 1205 and 1210 in York and was issued by the moneyer Davi (David) of Everwik (York).
Photographs courtesy of Hull City Museums and Art galleries.

Holderness, and his mastership, which lasted for fifteen years, was so successful that his supporters pleaded with him to provide an extra day of hunting. He apparently replied that with thirty couple (hounds) in kennel and only two horses fit to go by the end of the season, to do more than they were doing would require 'hounds of steel, horses of cast-iron and men of indiarubber'!

After Mr. Hodgson left, the hounds were sold to a Committee, forming the start of the Holderness Hunt. Among them was Mr. James Hall of Scorborough, who became Master in 1847 and remained in the position for thirty years. Under James Hall the hounds were once again kennelled at Etton where they have stayed until the present day. His hounds were described as being 'well-topped and full of bone' — some becoming founders of famous lines in other kennels.

Hall died in 1877 and there again followed a memorable mastership in the person of Mr. Arthur Wilson of Tranby Croft. His ability as a sportsman attracted a keen field, among them the Prince of Wales (the future King Edward VII), who joined the Hunt on several occasions. On 27 January 1882 the meet was at Brantinghamthorpe, the residence of Mr. Christopher Sykes, where the royal presence was reputed to have attracted 1,400 horsemen, 4,000 on foot and 1,000 in carriages!

During the late 1920s Major Newland Hillas of High Hall, Etton, became Joint Master with Captain Adrian Bethell of Rise Park. Just a few years later the Holderness country was divided; Mr. Hall of Walkington taking the Wold side, with a bitch pack of hounds kennelled at Etton, while Major Hillas and Captain Bethell continued to hunt the Holderness side from kennels at Rise Park, a mixed pack being lent to them by the Committee. The pack was reunited back at Etton in 1936, thus bringing the history of the hunt up to the Second World War.

At the outbreak of hostilities, hunting had to be abandoned and many good hounds were put down or dispersed, just a small nucleus being kept. Low Hall was taken over by the Army, and soldiers were billeted there for the duration of the war. But as soon as the war was over Major Hillas of High Hall once again took over the mastership. Lord Hotham and Mr. Anthony Bethell followed him as Joint Masters in 1952.[49]

Beaumont, Lord Hotham, acquired Low Hall from the Legard family in 1862 and it has remained as part of the Hotham estate to this day, the premises now being let to the Holderness Hunt. Name boards at the kennels record every Master of the Holderness Hunt from 1869 to the present day.

So, fox hunting in the area began over 250 years ago, with the village of Etton being closely involved for at least 150 years — a long association with a deep-rooted British tradition.

High Hall

High Hall is an 18th-century house, situated on the eastern side of Chantry Lane; a tall rambling building of red brick with stone dressings and shaped gables. It was much altered in the late 19th century by the Grimston family, who bought the house, with forty acres of land, in 1815, from Sarah Belt, wife of Leonard, the younger son of Robert and Elizabeth Belt. The property descended in the Grimston family until 1927, and it is their coat of arms which can be seen above the main entrance.[50]

During the time of Colonel and Mrs. Grimston's residence at High Hall from about 1865, several staff were employed, including a cook, kitchen maid, head housemaid, under housemaid, chauffeur and gardener.

It was compulsory for the maids, complete with their frilled white caps, to attend church on Sundays, and a special pew was reserved for them at the back of the church.

It was on returning from church one Sunday morning in 1898 that one of the maids, Gertrude Trinder, waved to a group of young men, one of whom had whistled to her. Colonel Grimston, a rather austere man, happened to spot her from a window at the Hall, summoned her to see him and promptly dismissed her from service. The young man who had caused her dismissal, Thomas Welbourn, was mortified and offered to marry her; an offer which she readily accepted.

Hounds are a familiar sight in the village of Etton. This photograph was taken at some time between 1907 and 1934 when the splendidly named J. Alexander Symington Mcloud Anderson was Head Kennelman. He can be seen in the foreground with Tom Stanley, the Whipper-in, at the rear. The Holderness Hunt Kennels are to the left of the picture and the old entrance pillars to the former gardens at the rear of Low Hall can just be made out in the wall at the end of the drive.

A recent photograph of the remains of Etton's 18th century tower windmill situated on the southern border of the parish. During the late 12th century Etton had a watermill but there were problems in maintaining a water supply powerful enough to drive the mill so, from about 1315, a windmill was sited on the hill east of the road to South Dalton. The last mention of a mill on this site was in 1712. It is thought that the present mill was built about 1775 to 1790. Thomas Roantree acquired the site in 1776 and George Roantree was recorded as 'miller' in 1838.

A story relating to the wife of one Etton miller tells that she insisted her husband should leave the bedroom at night through the window and then by ladder if the wind happened to be turning the sails at such a time. This prevented him from waking up the whole household by clumping down the stairs! See 'East Yorkshire Windmills' by Roy Gregory, 1985.

Photograph courtesy of Donald Innes Studios.

A hand-tinted photograph of St. Mary's Church, Etton, from the south-west, and dated c.1905. Note that the south porch was not added until 1926, being the gift of Mrs. Catherine Grimston of High Hall.
Reproduced by permission of Humberside Leisure Services (Beverley Local Studies Library).

This photograph was taken at Etton Kennels in about 1907. Charles Brook, Master 1905-8, arrives in an early motorcar, to be greeted by Col. J. B. Stracey Clitherow, Master c.1928.

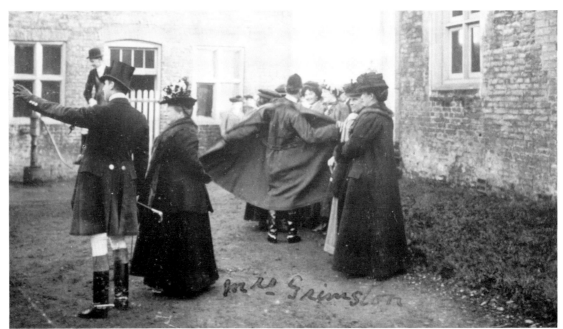

Mrs. Grimston, of High Hall, Etton, attends the meet at the kennels c.1907.

High Hall in 1800, from the south, looking vastly different from its appearance today. Sarah Belt, wife of Leonard, younger son of Robert and Elizabeth Belt, sold an estate of 40 acres, including High Hall, to Henry Grimston in 1815.

Taken in about 1898, this is one of the earliest photographs in the collection. It shows the staff who were employed at High Hall when Col. and Mrs. Grimston were in residence. Gertrude Trinder is standing on the right of the photograph –it was probably taken not long before she was dismissed.

High Hall (Etton Hall) from the south-east, taken in c.1905 when Catherine Grimston, widow of William Grimston, was in residence. It was they who altered and enlarged the Hall in the late 19th century. The chestnut tree on the left was removed in March, 1916 – it had obviously grown too large and was obscuring light from the house.
Photo courtesy of Humberside Leisure Services (Beverley Local Studies Library).

34

The Light Dragoon Inn.
An alehouse was recorded at Etton in about 1710 and a licensed house was listed in 1745 with two being mentioned in the late 18th century. By the 1820's there was just one licensed premises known as The Light Horseman and later called The Light Dragoon. During the 1840's a second public house existed – The Globe – but its situation is unknown.
Earlier this century, Lord Hotham's tenants would assemble at The Light Dragoon twice a year to pay their rents. It was quite a social occasion and the landlady would make spiced bread which was served along with a free drink.

A beautiful embroidered sampler, worked by Sarah Mason, aged 11 years, at Etton National School in 1860. This would have been the 'new' school building which was built just south of the church in 1855/56. On close inspection it can be seen that Sarah accidentally omitted the letter 'j' in the lower case line of the alphabet!
A small part of the field behind the whitewashed cottage opposite Ellerington Lane was once called Mason's Garth. Perhaps it was this cottage where Sarah's family lived – at one time it was divided into two tiny cottages, each with just one room upstairs, one room downstairs and a small dairy.

Mrs. Catherine Grimston, of High Hall, surrounded by village children after presenting mugs to celebrate the end of the First World War in 1918. Mrs. Grimston was a regular benefactor to the village and when she died in 1926 virtually the whole population of the village turned out to pay their last respects, such was their admiration for her.

Another staff group at High Hall, taken in the garden in about 1920. Horace Welbourn, gardener, is standing on the left and Mr. King, the head gardener, is seated. The poodle, Sammy, belonged to Mrs. Grimston.

The funeral cortège of Mrs. Catherine Grimston (d.1926), coming down Chantry Lane from High Hall. Mr. Thomas Welbourn, Mrs. Grimston's farm bailiff, is walking beside the wagon while his son, Cyril, leads the horses. Following her death, there was a three day auction sale at High Hall which attracted a large crowd including many strangers to the area.

Several years later, in 1915, after the Colonel had died, Mrs. Grimston appointed Thomas Welbourn as her farm bailiff, thereby setting right the mistake she felt her husband had made all those years before.

Home Farm, opposite what is now South Wolds School (formerly Etton Pasture School), belonged to High Hall and it was here that the Welbourn family came to live. The farm provided the Hall with produce to cater for the household and the lavish parties which were sometimes held there.

Besides the freshly churned butter and the cream which were sent to the Hall each week, 50lbs of butter was sent by horse-drawn carrier to market in Beverley. Also, there were at least 200 hens and 50 to 60 ducks kept on the farm to supply the kitchens at High Hall with both eggs and poultry.[51]

Catherine Grimston died in 1926 and High Hall was sold to Major Newland Hillas, a Joint Master of the Holderness Hunt. It was not to be many years until the Second World War intruded upon the well ordered life at High Hall. While soldiers were billeted at Low Hall (the hunt kennels), three army officers were sent to High Hall —country house life, with its numerous servants, would never be the same again.

Education

A schoolmaster was mentioned in Etton as early as 1791, and in 1819 there were two schools, both supported by subscriptions. One catered for between thirty-five and forty boys, the other for about thirty girls. A year later a National School began in a barn on the south side of Main Street.[52]

In 1855 William Musgrave (Rector 1854-78) wrote a letter[53] to the Council for Education in London:

The principal landed proprietor in the Parish is Lord Hotham M.P., who many years ago established a school for the inhabitants by fitting up an old barn for the purpose: The education here carried on is miserably deficient, and therefore little valued, the standard of attainment low, the attendance irregular and the discipline lax – and I am very anxious to put the whole thing on a higher footing. The site of the present school premises is low – surrounded with cottages and admits of no extension – I propose therefore to erect an entirely new set of commodious and well arranged school buildings with a teachers residence – there being none at present – on a small piece of rectorial glebe, about 1 rood in extent, most conveniently situated at one extremity of the village, adjacent to the Church and Rectory House.

The estimate of cost for the proposed buildings and fittings, including desks, pump and well etc. came to £750 15s.2d.[54]

On 1 November 1855 a meeting was held,[55] attended by Revd. W. P. Musgrave, H. E. Grimston Esq., Chairman, Revd. J. Gardner and Messrs. John Whipp, Thomas Whipp, Laurence Stevenson and John Wardell. It was resolved that 'it was at once desirable to elect a School-master and that his duties shall commence on the 1st January, 1856 in the Old School for the present.' A letter from the Training School, Battersea, recommending a Mr. Arthur Stote, aged 21 years, was read, and after much debate the committee agreed to his election and suggested £65 as his first year's salary. Hugh Roy was elected as a Pupil Teacher to work with Mr. Stote. It was common at this time for a bright senior pupil to become a pupil teacher, helping the other children while still receiving an education himself.

Rules for the governing of the school were drawn up and terms of payment by the parents of pupils agreed upon:

Agricultural and other Labourers to pay:

	s.	d		
for a single child	2.	0	*per quarter*	
" 2 children	3.	6	*"*	*"*
" 3 children	4.	0	*"*	*"*
and each additional child	1.	0	*"*	*"*
Farmers to pay for each child	6.	0	*"*	*"*

On 3 April 1857, one year after the opening of the new school, Mr. Stote gave his report:[56]

School photograph of 1906, taken in the kennels field with the school and church in the background. When the hunt met at the kennels, the children had a privileged view from the school playground. One of the greatest attractions was seeing the fine ladies riding side-saddle, their faces almost hidden by black veils.

Children from Etton School in 1914, taken outside the school with the Hunt Kennels in the background. Mr. Potts, the headmaster, can be seen standing on the right of the photograph. There were over 70 children at the school in the early 1920's, some of them coming from Gardham, Etton Wold and Etton Westwood. All the children walked to school and brought a packed lunch and cold tea in bottles. As time went by some of the children had bicycles and, to the envy of others, some had vacuum flasks for a hot drink. There were many odd jobs for the children to do which earned them a few pennies. There was milk to be fetched from the many cow owners, some of whom had their cows grazing on the pasture where South Wolds School now stands (formerly Etton Pasture Shool). Another useful occupation was for a reliable boy or girl to take the cows out to grass every morning and bring them back again for afternoon milking.

81 children have been admitted to the school during the year
The number on the book during the -

		average attendance
1st quarter was	*59*	*46*
2nd " "	*53*	*35*
3rd " "	*57*	*42*
4th " "	*67*	*55*

giving an average attendance of 44½.

This is a small average, but it is to be accounted for by the irregular attendance of many children just before and after harvest.

Many of the older children have left during the year, after having been but a few months at school. From such little can be expected, but they have generally learnt to write their names, and have improved a little in Reading, Spelling and Arithmetic.

Out of 81 children admitted during the past year only 19 could write their names.

The subjects now taught in the school are, Holy Scripture, Church Catechism, Liturgy, Writing, Arithmetic, Spelling, Composition, Geography, Grammar, English, History, Music; and Needlework (to the Girls).

Needlework was regarded as a vital skill for girls, 'sewing being a subject of such extreme importance to the future well being of the girls, more time should be attended to it (presently 3 hours a week).' In 1858 the School Inspector reported that 'the needlework is excellent, the elder girls cut out and make shirts entirely themselves; they are thorough seamstresses.'

In the headmaster's second report he bemoans the fact that he cannot receive the government capitation grant for children who do not attend school for 176 days or more in a year. 'A severe attack of Measles in October and November (1858) prevents many children from attending and several days are lost at the beginning of each quarter while parents consider whether they shall send their children or not.'

The Infant School opened on Monday 14 January 1858 in what was the old schoolroom, which is now more familiar in Etton as the Village Hall. They stayed there until about 1875, then transferred to the new school, where additional accommodation had to be provided for them in 1915.

Relationships with parents in the village seemed to become strained, and in 1863 Mr. Stote resigned after reporting that confrontation between parents and himself was undermining discipline. Several years later, in 1901, a letter was sent by Revd. Cockin (Rector 1894-1908) to Mr. Hindley, Schoolmaster, about 'punishments of detention given to children for failure to attend school — the parents in the village being irritated by this.'

In the winter of 1906 the school had to close for a whole month due to an outbreak of Scarlet Fever. The school, nevertheless, obviously flourished for many years until, in 1955, senior pupils were transferred to Beverley. The school closed completely in 1966, children from Etton subsequently going to Cherry Burton.

Reading Room

The old infant school, which closed in about 1875, re-opened as a Parish Reading Room on February 14 1876. Newspapers and books were made available to subscribers and a list of rules was drawn up by the organising committee.[57]

1. All subscribers of 1s. quarterly shall be entitled to the use of the Reading Room, and be considered members.

2. Any parishioner of Etton, not a member, shall be allowed to use the room on payment of 2d. a week.

3. Every member shall have the privilege of introducing a stranger or non-parishioner for one night.

4. The Rector or his Curate shall be permitted to hold a meeting or service in the room on giving 24 hours' notice.

5. No gambling whatsoever shall be allowed.

6. Any member entering the Reading Room in a state of intoxication, or guilty of swearing and using profane language, shall be fined 6d. and on his refusal to pay that fine,

This happy group of schoolchildren was photographed in about 1926. The teachers are Miss Hardy (left) and Mrs. Saynor, the headmistress (right). The children can be identified as:

Back Row (left to right): ? Gladys Haines, Ethel Cooper, Doris Teal, Enid Spear, Biddy Haines, Betty Starkey, Violet Parker, Ida Atkins, Mary Huzzard

Middle Row (left to right): Billy Haines, Herbert Witty, Ken Hill, George Waudby, David Dalby, John Bugg, Bobby Dewsbury, Ron Hardwick

Front Row (left to right): Bobby Deighton, Alec Anderson, Kitty Deighton, Vera Baxter, Walter Atkins, Charlie Parker (nearly hidden), Ivy Baxter, Molly Bugg, Ernest Bugg, Arthur Dalby.

This photograph was taken in 1964, just two years before the school finally closed.
Back Row (left to right): Mr. Sykes, Freda Tough, Pauline Hobson, Claire Robinson, Denise Bennett,
Gillian Baxter, Ann Spence, Miss Taylor.
Middle Row (left to right): Keith Marshall, Barry Hill, Stuart Rennie, Graham Marshall, Geoffrey Turner,
James Tough, Ian Tough, Neville Hodgson.
Front Row (left to right): Karen Spence, Neil Marshall, Annabell Robinson, Lorraine Hales, Christine Rawdon, William Hobson,
Graham Hales, Jennifer Tough, Anthony Hobson, Lesley Palmer.

This photograph shows the children from Etton School taking their harvest gifts to the church just before the school closed in 1966. They are, from left to right:
William Hobson, Jane Hobson, Jennifer Tough, Linda Morrell, Lorraine Hales, Neil Marshall, Karen Spence, Graham Hales, Graham Hill, Christine Rawdon, Anthony Hobson, Keith Marshall, Freda Tough, Miss Taylor and Mrs. Huzzard.
Photograph by Mary Varley.

43

or on a repetition of the offence, he shall cease to be a member.

7. *No one shall retain possession of a newspaper more than twenty minutes if it is wanted by another member.*

8. *No one under fourteen years of age can be admitted a member of the Reading Room.*

In 1895 the building had to be completely refurbished. According to a newspaper report of the time:[58]

> *The most important part of the work has been the creation of an entirely new roof. The roof is covered with flat red tiles and boarded on the inside with varnished pine boards, which give a very handsome appearance to the rooms. A brick wall divides the building into two rooms, measuring inside 28ft by 15ft and 14ft by 15ft respectively. The smaller room has been also much improved by the insertion of a bay window, the gift of Mrs. Grimston, of Etton High Hall.*

These alterations and improvements came to the princely sum of £85.

During the Second World War the Reading Room became the local Air Raid Warden's post, accommodating the warden, two firemen and a home guard. Following this the building came into use as a Young Men's Club, with a billiards room on one side and a reading room on the other.

Eventually, the building fell into disuse and, after several years and much fund-raising, a Village Hall Committee, originally founded in 1942, bought the premises from the Church for £250. Once again, the building was altered. The interior dividing wall and the bay window were removed and a kitchen extension added. So in about 1970, after well over one hundred years of village use, the premises were again opened to the community, this time as a Village Hall.[59]

The Village Population

In 1662, Parliament passed an Act for a tax to be levied on the number of domestic hearths in a house. Several returns were made by local officers, recording the hearths belonging to parishioners in Etton, from that time, until the repeal of the Act in 1688.

The Hearth Tax Returns for Etton in 1672 list 68 households, with 48 having one hearth, 14 with two, 2 with three, 3 with four to eight and 1 with fifteen — the last mentioned being Low Hall, now Etton Kennels. Geoffrey Blacktoller, Rector 1666-76, is listed as having six hearths at the Rectory. Twenty-five households were exempted from the tax.[60]

There were 55 families in the parish in 1743 and 41 in 1764. In 1801 the population was 321 rising to 502 in 1861 and decreasing to 398 in 1891[61]. On the last page of Etton Register No.4[62] is the following entry:

> *March 10th 1801 – By an Order of Parliament an Account of the Number of Houses, Families and Inhabitants of the Parish of Etton, was accurately taken and was then found to be as follows:*

Houses	Families	Males	Females	Inhabitants
55	68	167	154)	
			167)	321

In Agriculture	*Trades and Handicrafts*
80	21

People belonging to neither of the above classes – 220.

In 1838, Revd. Machell (Curate-in-charge) recorded the full details of his parishioners, giving the name of the head of each household, their Title, Quality or Calling, the number of children and the number of menservants, womenservants and apprentices. A total of 79 households were listed[63] with 411 people living or employed in the village. Among those listed were:

> *Thomas Spence – Farmer of Wallis Grange*
> *2 children, 9 menservants, 3 womenservants*
>
> *Thomas Whipp Senior – Farmer*
> *3 children, 12 menservants, 3 womenservants*
>
> *Mrs. Jane Legard (High Hall) – Gentlewoman*
> *1 manservant, 3 womenservants*

This photograph was taken outside the Reading Room (Village Hall), c.1911, on what is thought to be the occasion of the Odd Fellows Club Feast, The Club Feast was a truly festive event, with swings, roundabouts and stalls being set up in the field next to the pond, and a marquee being erected for the actual feast. George Hill can be seen standing, with crutches and foot sling, to the left of the picture, with Charles Sever next to him, his hand resting on George's shoulder. Joe Orvis, Horace Welbourn (Etton's last Postmaster), Arthur Bugg and Tom Whipp can be seen standing around them. The gentleman wearing the bowler hat, towards the centre of the picture, is Mr. T. Whipp, Tom's father. On the right of the photograph there is a beautifully decorated ice-cream cart.

Etton Fire Crew - 1939/40 - based at the Village Hall (then the Reading Room) during the Second World War. It shows left to right: Jim Kitchen, Tom Long, Robert Spence, George Starkey, Doug Hardy, Sam Starkey, Alan Spence, Cyril Welbourn, Norman Spear and Ken Hill.

William Jackson – Etton Wold
4 children, 6 menservants, 1 womanservant
Robert Machell – Clergyman
8 children, 4 womenservants

Among the rest there were 3 cordwainers (shoemakers/leather workers), 2 carpenters, a bricklayer, a butcher, a blacksmith, a tailor and a miller. Mary Moore was the shopkeeper, Miss Brookelbank the schoolmistress, George Theakstone the schoolmaster, Christopher Goodricke the publican and the remaining parishioners were mostly farmers and labourers.

Revd. Machell also recorded numerous interestng facts in the parish registers[64] of the mid 19th century. Victorian families were often very large and evidence of this can be found in his notes. On recording the death of Ann Wainer in 1839, age 48 years, he wrote that 'she died 2 days after giving birth to her 15th child from grief at the misconduct of one of her daughters, who had left her place and gone with the soldiers'. (Soldiers were often billeted in villages when they were on manoeuvres through the country). Of his own wife, Eliza Mary Machell, who died in 1841, age 39 years, he wrote that her death followed the birth of her 12th child, 10 of whom survived; the newly born child died just 6 weeks later. He tenderly recorded that they had been happily married for 20 years.

Many deaths in the 19th century were from Consumption (Tuberculosis), Cholera, Typhoid Fever and Scarlet Fever. In just one year, in 1835, seven children in Etton, aged between 2 and 8 years, died from Scarlet Fever. Poverty was rife during this time and in the same year two people died from excessive alcohol consumption, perhaps to drown their sorrows due to their reduced circumstances.

In the Register of Baptisms for the period 1813-64, Revd. Machell placed a 'B' or 'B5/-' next to the names of children from poor families in the parish. He explained at the foot of one of the pages that '"B" signifies 'Blanket' — Give a five shilling blanket to those who are thus marked. 'B5/-' signifies — That give the money instead if the parties like it better. This and forgiving them their Churching Fee helps the poor a little." An average of thirteen blankets a year were given out in the 1840's.

Etton was a self-sufficient village community and this is well illustrated by the following list of notable residents, tradesmen and farmers, taken from Bulmer's 'History and Directory of East Yorkshire — 1892'.

Post Office at John Shaw's. Letters, *via* Hull, arrive at 7.15 a.m.; and are despatched at 5.35 p.m. No Sunday business.

Ash George,	huntsman, The Kennels
Brigham Joseph,	corn miller
Burgess Straker,	carrier to Beverley (Sat.)
Burnaby Rev. John Charles Wellesley, M.A.,	The Rectory
Cooper Geo.,	blacksmith, and steam thrashing machine proprietor
Dalby David,	first whip
Dewsbury George	
Dosser Mark Brown,	saddler
Ellerington William,	shoemaker
Gabbetis Elizabeth,	Light Dragoon Inn
Gabbetis George Edward,	butcher
Goodricke Mrs. Charlotte,	grocer
Grimston Wm. Henry, Esq., J.P.,	High Hall
Harper John,	carrier to Hull (Tuesday) and Beverley (Saturday)
Hill George,	wheelwright & joiner
Holderness Hounds,	The Kennels — Arthur Wilson, Esq., master, Tranby croft; Geo. Ash, huntsman; Wm. Shaw, stud groom
Hornby Walter,	station master, N.E.R., Kipling Cotes
Horsfield Wm.,	shoemaker
Huzzard William Wilkinson,	market gardener, parish clerk, registrar of births and deaths, and vaccination officer for Lockington district of Beverley Union
National School;	O. W. Wilkins, master
Scruton Robert,	tailor and draper
Shaw John,	shopkeeper and postmaster
Shaw William,	stud groom
Welbourn Richard,	tailor
West George,	carrier and sexton

Farmers

Askwith John,	Manor House
Gabbetis William	
Grant Messrs. William and John,	Hornby
Hardy George William (hind to Col. Grimston),	Lodge Farm
Jackson John,	Westwood House

Jackson Robert,	Etton field
Jackson Thomas,	Top House farm
Langdale John R.	Walk farm
Shaw Samuel	(yeo.)
Spence Miss	
Frances Ann,	Wallace grange
Welbourn Robert	(and bricklayer and builder)
Whipp Thomas	
Wood John	

The village of Etton remained virtually unchanged until after the Second World War with hardly any needs to be satisfied from outside.

The population in 1988 was recorded as 280[65], with many of the residents employed in Beverley and Hull in varying occupations quite unrelated to Etton's agricultural heritage. However, there still remains a strong agricultural foundation in the parish and as long as this exists, the village will retain its rather individual character, slightly set apart from the hustle and bustle of the modern world.

REFERENCES

1. From exhibition notes by Adrian Havercroft, archaeological executor for the late Prof. W. J. Varley.
2. Ibid.
3. *Forty years Research in British and Saxon Burials in East Yorkshire*, Mortimer 1907.
4. See note 1.
5. V.C.H. East Riding Vol. IV p.107.
6. P.R.O. E142/16-18 (Latin).
7. Ex inf. Mrs. M. Varley.
8. Kenrick's Archaeological and Historical Papers —1864. Chapter 1 *The Rise and Suppression of the Order of the Knights Templar in Yorkshire*. H.L.S.L.
9. Ibid. See also *The Knights Templars in England*, Thomas W. Parker (Tuscon 1965).
10. Calendar of Close Rolls—Edward II 1307-13 p. 400. H.L.S.L.
11. See note 1.
12. *Etton – An East Yorkshire Village – 1170-1482*. T. Walter Hall. (J. W. Northend 1932).
13. V. C. H. East Riding Vol. IV p. 108.
14. See note 12.
15. V. C. H. East Riding Vol. IV p. 109-110.
16. Located by Prof. W. J. Varley.
17. V. C. H. East Riding Vol. IV p. 105. *Etton – An East Yorks Village*.
18. H. U. L. DDCV — 53/1.
19. H. R. O. PE 52/9.
20. V. C. H. East Riding Vol. IV p. 110.
21. H. R. O. PC/28/1.
22. V. C. H. East Riding Vol. IV p. 107.
23. H. U. L. DDHO 30/93.
24. To the nearest whole acre. Ex. inf. Mr. A. Wilson
25. H. R. O. PE 52/43.
26. Etton Terrier 1817 H. R. O. PE 52/40.
27. V. C. H. East Riding Vol. IV p. 112.
28. See Foster's *Pedigrees of Yorkshire* Vol. III. B. L. S. L.
29. H. R. O. PE 52/5.
30. Ex. inf. Mr. A. Lathrop U. S. A.
31. Ex. inf. Mrs. T. W. Kilian U. S. A.
32. See note 30.
33. V. C. H. East Riding Vol. IV p. 113.
34. H. R. O. PE 52/1.
35. Ex inf. Rev. D. Austerberry, Kinnerley, Oswestry.
36. See board in St. Mary's Church, Etton.
37. H. R. O. PE 52/43.
38. H. R. O. PE 52/66/3.
39. Ex inf. Mr. B. S. R. Rambaut.
40. B. I. H. R. TER I Etton 1685.
41. *Historical & Architectural survey of Etton Rectory* by Mr. S. Robson — Private Collection.
42. See note 40.
43. B. I. H. R. TER I Etton 1764.
44. H. R. O. PE 52/40 Terrier 1817.
45. Extract from newspaper report — H. R. O. PE 52/50.
46. See note 41.
47. V. C. H. East Riding Vol. IV p. 107.
48. Ibid p. 105.
49. *A Short History of the Holderness Hunt* Ralph Greaves c.1951.
50. V. C. H. East Riding Vol. IV p. 109.
51. Ex inf. Misses M. & A. Welbourn.
52. V. C. H. East Riding Vol. IV p. 114.
53. H. R. O. PE 52/76.
54. Ibid.
55. H. R. O. PE 52/70 — PE 52/74 School records.
56. Ibid.
57. Parish News March 1876 — part of periodical *Home Words*.
58. H. R. O. PE 52/51.
59. Ex inf. Mr. E. Bugg.
60. V. C. H. East Riding Vol. IV p. 106.
61. V. C. H. Yorkshire Vol. II.
62. H. R. O. PE 52/4.
63. H. R. O. PE 52/44.
64. H. R. O. PE 52/5 and PE 52/9.
65. Based on Registrar General's estimate.

V. C. H.   = Victoria County History
P. R. O.   = Public Record Office, London
H. U. L.   = Hull University Library
H. R. O.   = Humberside Record Office, Beverley
B. I. H. R. = Borthwick Institute of Historical Research, York
B. L. S. L. = Beverley Local Studies Library
H. L. S. L. = Hull Local Studies Library

Prof. Varley's notes and drawings placed with the Royal Commission on Historic Buildings, London.

5

Lot
59 Set of pillar and claw dining tables, in three parts, 7 feet 6 inches long, and 4 feet 6 inches wide
60 Ten mahogany chairs and two arm ditto, hair bottoms, brafs nailed
61 Two back fcreens
62 Quadrant pat cupboard
63 Ditto
64 Dumb waiter
65 Ditto
66 Pair of mahogany library fteps
67 A feven-bottle wine cooper, brafs hoop'd
68 Folding fire fcreen
69 Scotch carpet, 6 yards by 5¼
70 Green wire fender, brafs top
71 Featherbed, bolfter and two pillows
72 Three fingle blankets, one white counterpane
73 Wire fender
74 Mahogany cheefe cradle, two waiters
75 Two tin buckets and covers
76 Four bed lamps
77 Six flat candlefticks
78 Pair of brafs ditto fnuffers and ftand
79 Mahogany dining tray
80 Ditto
81 Mahogany oval tea tray
82 Ditto
83 Wine cooper
84 Dreffing glafs
85 Two mahogany knife trays
86 Japan ditto and bread bafket
87 Two card racks
88 Two green moreen curtains
89 A gentleman's tool cheft
90 Fender and fire irons
91 Tin lanthorn, patent lamp and bracket
92 Iron footman and hanging iron
93 Six prints, framed
94 Two watering pans

Second Day's Sale.

Lot
1 DRIPPING pan and iron ftand
2 Morter and peftel
3 Three turnip fcoups and an apple coarer
4 Carrot fcoup, fix tin pots, covers and ftands
5 Sugar nippers, flour box and pepper box
6 Cullender and two iron frying pans
7 Two boxes of pafte cutters
8 Five fmall fpoons, foup ladle and large grater
9 Bafting ladle and two fkimmers
10 One amlet pan, two tart ditto
11 Twenty-four round patty pans
12 Two fifh kettles, covers and plates
13 One brazin pan, cover and plate
14 Three foup plates and covers
15 Three ftew pans and covers
16 Ditto
17 Ditto
18 Ditto
19 Three faucepans and covers
20 Ditto
21 Two fquare baking plates
22 One round cutler pan
23 Two large moulds
24 Twelve fmall fluited
25 Twelve ditto plain
26 Cheefe toafter plate and cover
27 Kitchen fender
28 Cafe of larding pins
29 Large pot and cover
30 Water boiler and ditto
31 Turn-up bedftead
32 Featherbed, bolfter and one pillow
33 Mattrafs
34 Three blankets and a rug
35 Large deal linen prefs
36 Handfome japan plate warmer

7

Lot
37 Tea urn, plated mouldings
38 Coffee urn,   ditto
39 Commode fender

ATTIC-ROOM.

40 Oval box glafs and toilet table
41 Commode cafe of mahogany drawers
42 Bafon ftand, with covers and tambore door
43 Mahogany writing table, double horfe
44 Ditto library table
45 Biddet ftool
46 Two Bruffe's bedfide carpets
47 High wire fender and brufh
48 Mahogany dreffing table, knee hole front
49 Ditto cafe of drawers
50 Swing glafs
51 Deal prefs bedftead painted
52 Mahogany card table unlined
53 Ditto breakfaft table
54 Featherbed, bolfter and two pillows
55 One palliafs
56 Portable writing defk
57 Three blankets and one cotton counterpane

HORSES.

58 One crop'd bay mare, 7 years old
59 A bay horfe, 6 years old
60 Ditto ftallion, 7 years old
61 A chefnut horfe, 5 years old
62 A black horfe, aged
63 A bay mare, aged
64 Ladies fide faddle and bridle
65 Ditto
66 Man's faddle and bridle
67 Ditto
68 Ditto
69 Ditto
70 Ditto

Part of a Sale Catalogue giving details of the household contents, belonging to the Hon. Colonel Rawdon, which were sold at auction on the premises, at Etton, on Wednesday, 8th June, 1796 and also on the two following days. It was obviously a sizeable property which included a cellar and stables but its situation in the village is unknown.

The Catalogue runs to several pages, so only a few are reproduced here, but in its entirety it reveals that Col. Rawdon was undoubtedly prosperous, keeping a well stocked cellar of no less than 1,596 bottles of choice wines!
Reproduced by kind permission of the Humberside Record Office. Ref. H.R.O. DDBD 22/1.

This photograph of Church Farm (c.1905), taken from an old postcard, shows St. Mary's Church to the right and, in the rear centre, two conical hay stacks, known as 'pikes', which were the speciality of Joe Allen. He would, apparently, go and stand up on the Cherry Burton Road to check that the stacks were perfectly symmetrical. The farm buildings have hardly changed since the photograph was taken.
Photo courtesy of Humberside Leisure Services (Beverley Local Studies Library).

A photograph taken at the junction of Main Street and the Cherry Burton road, with the war memorial and the Village Hall (then the Reading Room) on the left. The white cottage, side on to the road on the right, was demolished after the Second World War. The car and van date the photograph to about 1935.

THE LAST LOAD

Entitled 'The Last Load', this photograph was taken outside 'Cherry Corner' during the first quarter of this century. It shows, standing in the foreground: 1st right, Herbert Harper, gardener at the Hall; 2nd right, Mr. Bolton, Kennelman; 4th right, ? Arthur Bugg. Others unknown.

Life in Etton at this time was much simpler and conducted at a more gentle pace than it is today. Most cottages had a pig sty and so kept a pig or two. In winter the pigs were killed (Mr. Appleton was the pig killer) and that meant delicious sausages, black puddings, pork pies, spare ribs and scraps. Pig frys were shared out amongst friends. Later, brawn was made and much later the bacon and ham, which was salted, was hung from ceiling hooks ready for use.

On Saturday mornings, the highlight was to look out for the carrier (in early 1920's, Mr. Moss) going from Dalton to Beverley, who would shop for anything that was needed and possibly bring back any parcel that relatives might have left for him to deliver on his way back at teatime, for the princely sum of sixpence (2½p!).

This watery scene could hardly be identified today as being Etton's village pond. The cottages, although still there, have been rebuilt and the succulent growths of wild rhubarb surrounding the pond have long since disappeared. Just out of the picture, on the left, there was a pump, one of several which were in the village and still used up until about 1934 when the Dalton Estate laid on piped water into the village for a small payment. Before this the village children were often given the job of fetching fresh drinking water from the various pumps and wells.

This photograph, taken near the village pond, dates to some time early this century. The cottages behind the pond are just visible, but whether the tree came down in a storm or was deliberately felled, is not known. The old man in the centre of the photograph, with the fluffy white beard, has been identified as Straker Burgess, the man who was addicted to horseradish! It is thought that the man standing behind the tree trunk is Mr. George Appleton, father of Robert, and listed in Kelly's Directory of 1921 as a 'carting contractor, assistant overseer and clerk to the Parish Council.'

This picture shows the Village Shop, next to the Village Hall. It was owned by Mr. H. Wright in the 1920s and was later run by the Welbourn family when it was also a Post Office.
Jars of sweets are on shelves inside the window and the notice above the door on the left reads 'To Cylists – Refreshments Available Here – Tea, Coffee Etc.' Mrs. Wright used to bake bread which she sold in the shop and their daughter was an infant teacher at Etton Village School.

Taken just after the First World War, this shows the newly erected war memorial. Standing, from the left, are Phyllis Walton with her brother Frank, Dorothy Anderson, Mrs. Danby, (unknown), Nora Danby, Mrs. Teal, Annie Danby and Florie Midgeley.

54

A thatched house on the south side of Main Street at the turn of the century. On close inspection, the property can be seen to be in a considerable state of decay, with crumbling walls and chimney stack. The outline of the eaves and the old brickwork of the house can still be seen in the side wall of 45 Main Street. The old lady standing in the doorway, Mrs. Stewartson, seems to be the focus of attention for the children.

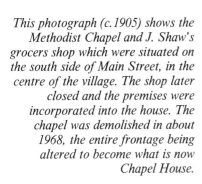

This photograph (c.1905) shows the Methodist Chapel and J. Shaw's grocers shop which were situated on the south side of Main Street, in the centre of the village. The shop later closed and the premises were incorporated into the house. The chapel was demolished in about 1968, the entire frontage being altered to become what is now Chapel House.

A photograph of the centre of the village, looking westwards, c.1930-40. White House Farm is on the left, with Manor House Farm and the Methodist Chapel next to it. A lone chicken struts in the middle of the road somehow giving emphasis to an otherwise solitary scene. Motor vehicles were still a comparative rarity in the village.

Another thatched property, on the north side of Main Street, looking west (c.1905). Since demolished, this is now the entrance to 82 Main Street. The cottage abutting the street next to it was occupied by a Mr. Straker Burgess. He was reputed to be quite strange as he never wore socks and ate horseradish (which he grew himself in plenty) by the bowlful.

This shows the saddler and cobbler's wooden hut, which was situated at the site of 84 Main Street at the turn of the century and up to about 1940. The owner, Mr. Waites, is standing outside his shop, surrounded by the tack used for heavy farm horses. The young boy in the centre is Charles Sever and in the rear centre of the picture, hardly visible, is the butcher's horse and cart which belonged to Mr. Meadley of Beverley.

Mr. Waites cycled from his home in Lund every day until he retired and his shop became a popular meeting place for the older village gentlemen. When he retired the hut was taken down and delivered on a tractor to his home in Lund. The hut stands in the same garden in Lund to this day.

On the right of this photograph is the blacksmith's workshop which was demolished in 1991. The white cottage next to it, once occupied by the Appleton family, was demolished in c.1966 and replaced with a modern house. The fabric of this cottage is interesting in that it was the only building left in the village built almost entirely of stone. It is thought that these chalk stones may have come from the Templar site in the village. The gabled house, now known as Wold Cottage, was where the village tailor, Tom Scruton, lived and worked earlier this century. The cottage abutting the pavement, in the centre of the picture, has now been altered and greatly extended.

This photograph shows Eric Thompson, Etton's last village blacksmith, working at his anvil some years ago. The blacksmith's house still stands and has recently been modernised and extended, but the workshops have now been demolished.
Photograph by Mary Varley.

A group of farm workers at Gardham c.1920 (part of Gardham lies within the parish of Etton). It is interesting to see just how many people were employed on a farm at this time – very different from the numbers today. Some of the men in the photograph came from Etton, including 5 Kitchen brothers – Jim, Joe, George, Harry and Walker.

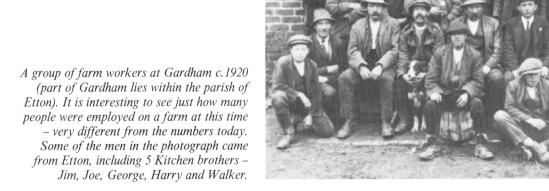

This photograph, taken in 1920, shows the villagers assembled for the Methodist Anniversary, always a grand affair, which was held in the barns at Laburnum Farm. This picture was actually taken where the sports were held, on land farmed by Mr. Jackson (of Bank House Farm) at the back of where the bungalows now stand. The Wood family were then at Laburnum Farm and they and the Hills, who provided the trestle tables for the tea, were allowed in free of charge. Those who did not belong to the Methodist Chapel had to pay 6d.

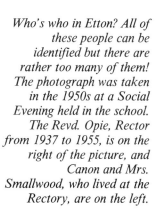

Who's who in Etton? All of these people can be identified but there are rather too many of them! The photograph was taken in the 1950s at a Social Evening held in the school. The Revd. Opie, Rector from 1937 to 1955, is on the right of the picture, and Canon and Mrs. Smallwood, who lived at the Rectory, are on the left.

List of Subscribers

Susan Ainley
Mrs. Armstrong
Rev. D. Austerberry
L. Aye-Maung
J. Barnes
N. Neal
Mrs. E. Bell
Stuart M. Bell
H. A. Birch
Pat & Russ Bolger
Sally Boston
Mr. H. Bottomley
Mr. R. Broadley
C. R. Brown
Miss J. Bugg
Thelma M. Bugg
Mr. T. H. Bugg
K. Cigno
Mr. & Mrs. P. Clapham
Joseph Clark
Mrs. A. Chisnall
Mrs. M. Cunliffe
M. K. Dunling
Mr. & Mrs. A. Eggleston
Janet Ellicott
Mr. & Mrs. G. Farmer
Suzanne M. Farr
Bernard Gerrard
Mrs. S. Gibson
John & Helen Gill
Alan Green
L. H. Green
Nicola Hallett
Mr. & Mrs. G. Harrison
C. S. Harrod

Jean Rogers Haws
J. E. Heslop
Mrs. J. Hill
P. Houghton
L. Howell
R. Hurst
Mrs. R. James
Mrs. B. D. Johnson
Mrs. L. Johnson
Mr. & Mrs. J. Jolliffe
Mrs. J. E. G. Jones
Joan Kemp
Geoff Kirk
Eric Kitchen
Mr. & Mrs. H. J. Langton
Ann & Arthur Lathrop
Victoria Lavin
C. P. A. Lown
P. J. Lown
Kenneth McKenzie
Miss B. Marginson
D. Marshall
Mrs. J. Marshall
Mr. & Mrs. A. Maskell
Mrs. Maggie Menzies
Mrs. Morrell
Rebecca Moverley
Mr. & Mrs. R. Moverley
Marjorie Potter
R. W. Price
Mr. & Mrs. B. S. R. Rambaut
P. R. Rambaut
Mrs. I. Rawlins
Mr. & Mrs. A. Rennie
C. Robinson

Mr. & Mrs. H. Robinson
Mrs. M. R. Rowell
Revd. Fr. Geoffrey P. Selby
Miss E. & M. Sever
Mr. & Mrs. R. Sharp
Mrs. M. Sleight
Brenda Smith
Mr. & Mrs. R. Spence
Mr. & Mrs. R. Stocks
J. P. Suhs
Helen Lathrop Taber
William Stevens Taber, Jnr.
David Lathrop Taber
Mrs. E. Thompson
Eric Thompson
R. Thompson
Mrs. M. E. Walker
Mr. W. Ward
Mr. & Mrs. P. Watts
Wilma Lathrop Waugh
Mr. D. Welbourn
Mr. Howard Welbourn
M. Welbourn
Mr. & Mrs. G. White
Mr. & Mrs. J. White
P. E. Widd
Rev. Bob Wilkinson
Mr. & Mrs. H. Wilkinson
Darren Williamson
Sally Wilson
Sylvia Winkle
Richard Yeo